The Wright Brothers

Robyn O'Sullivan

Contents

Wilbur Wright looks on as his brother successfully flies their airplane, *Flyer.*

The Age of Flight

Something amazing happened on the beach at Kitty
Hawk, North Carolina, on December 17, 1903.
Two brothers were on the beach that morning.
They had a flying machine they had built themselves.
Orville Wright took off in the machine. He flew a
distance of 120 feet in the air before landing again.
It was the world's first successful airplane flight.

Flyer makes history as the first powered airplane to take flight.

The Wright brothers' airplane, *Flyer*, was **powered** by an engine. The pilot lay on the bottom wing next to the engine. He steered the airplane with a **lever** and wires. He was able to make the airplane go up and down. He was also able to control the direction in which it flew.

Orville's flight was 10 feet above the ground and lasted just 12 seconds. He and his brother, Wilbur, made three more flights that morning. During the last flight, Wilbur flew the airplane a distance of 852 feet in 59 seconds. On December 17, 1903, the age of flight was born.

TELEGRAPH

Success. Four flights Thursday morning... with engine power alone. Average speed through air nearly 31 miles. Longest 57 seconds. Inform press. Home Christmas.

The Wright brothers sent a telegraph to their father telling him about their success. The telegraph operator made a mistake by typing the number "57" instead of "59."

Chapter 1
How It All Began

Wilbur Wright was born in 1867. Orville was born four years later. They grew up in Dayton, Ohio. They had two older brothers and a younger sister.

When Wilbur and Orville were boys, their father bought them a toy helicopter. The helicopter was powered by a twisted rubber band. The boys were amazed that it could fly through the air.

Wilbur at the age of thirteen   **Orville at the age of nine**

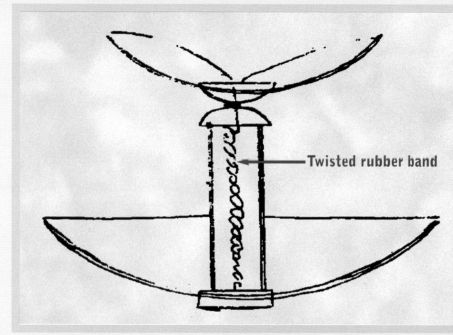

Twisted rubber band

Orville drew a diagram of the toy helicopter.

Their parents had always encouraged them to be curious about how things worked. The boys made copies of the toy helicopter. They figured out how to make them fly. Playing with toy helicopters sparked Wilbur and Orville's interest in flight.

In 1892, Wilbur and Orville became interested in bicycles. They soon began to repair bicycles for their friends. They opened a bicycle shop where they built their own bicycles.

Wilbur and Orville Wright built and sold bicycles in this bicycle shop.

In 1896, Wilbur read about Otto Lilienthal. This man was also interested in making a flying machine. He had made 2,000 flights in hang gliders in Germany. The brothers began to read everything they could find about flying.

The Wright brothers were very interested in Otto Lilienthal's hang gliders.

Chapter 2

Controlled Flight

By the 1890s, many people had tried to build flying machines. All of these people faced two problems. How could they get the machine off the ground? How could they control the machine in the air? The Wright brothers decided that control was the biggest problem. They realized a machine would crash if it couldn't be kept steady in the air.

This early flying machine was unable to get off the ground.

Wilbur had noticed that some birds twisted the tips of their wings when they flew. This kept the birds from being blown about by the wind. The brothers built a kite with two sets of wings. Any flying machine with two wings is called a **biplane**. The wings on the biplane kite could be twisted using wires. Wilbur controlled the kite by twisting its wings.

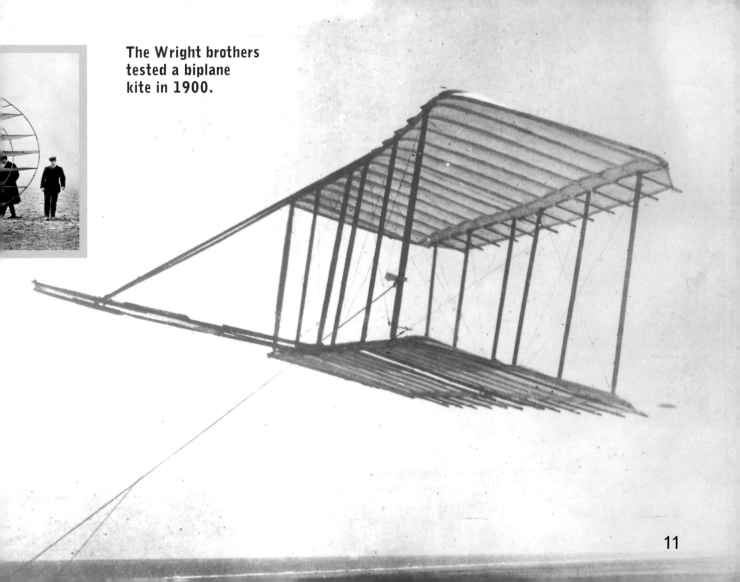

The Wright brothers
tested a biplane
kite in 1900.

11

Wilbur lies on the bottom wing of the glider.

The next step was to build a biplane **glider** big enough to carry a pilot. While they were working on the glider, Wilbur wrote to the U.S. Weather Bureau. He wanted to find a place with strong winds where they could test their glider. The Bureau suggested Kitty Hawk, a small town on the coast of North Carolina.

Two men held each side of the glider and ran until it lifted up into the air.

In 1900, Wilbur and Orville traveled to Kitty Hawk to test their glider. First, they flew it like a kite. Each brother controlled the wires on one wing. Then, Wilbur piloted the glider. He was able to control the glider as it flew! In the next two years the brothers returned many times to Kitty Hawk. They tested changes they had made to their gliders.

A Wind Tunnel

Wilbur and Orville needed to test which wing shapes flew best. To do this, they built a wind tunnel. The wind tunnel was a long wooden box with a fan at one end. The fan made a wind of about 30 miles per hour in the box. They tested different shaped wings in the wind tunnel. The wind tunnel was a great success. The brothers were able to test over 200 different wings.

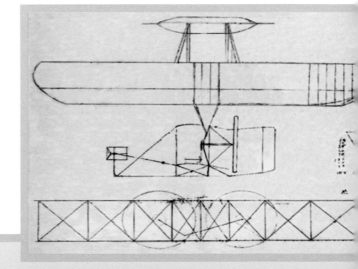

This is a diagram of one of the airplanes made by the Wright brothers.

The glass window let the brothers see how the wings were moving in the wind tunnel.

The brothers placed a fan at this end of the tunnel.

The brothers placed models of different wing shapes inside the tunnel at this end.

Wilbur and Orville discovered a problem with their gliders. They found they could only fly in a straight line. As soon as they tried to turn the glider left or right, they lost control. Wilbur and Orville learned that they needed to add a **rudder**, or tail, at the back of the airplane. This would help the pilot to turn the airplane.

In October 1902, Wilbur and Orville went to Kitty Hawk to test their third glider. They made about 1,000 flights in the new glider. Soaring in the skies over Kitty Hawk, the Wright brothers learned to fly!

Wilbur Wright pilots the third glider they made.

Chapter 3

Powered Flight

Now that they could control a flying machine, Wilbur and Orville began to think about how to power it. They thought about using an automobile engine, but these engines were too heavy.

Their bicycle mechanic, Charlie Taylor, helped them build a lighter engine. It took them six weeks to build the engine. It took them three months to design and build **propellers**. The propellers helped make the airplane move forward.

At last, the Wright Brothers were ready to build their first airplane. They took their plane to Kitty Hawk. On December 17, 1903, Orville made the world's first manned, powered airplane flight.

Charlie Taylor helped the Wright brothers build an engine for their airplane.

The brothers made three more flights that day. After the last flight, a strong wind smashed *Flyer* into the ground. The airplane was never flown again.

The Wright brothers placed this engine in their airplane.

The Wright brothers made four successful flights in *Flyer*.

The Pilot Is in Control

Wilbur and Orville's first airplane was a biplane called *Flyer*.

1 An **elevator** moved the airplane up or down. The pilot used a lever to move the elevator.

2 The **wing wires** allowed the pilot to twist the wings.

3 The **rudder**, or tail, at the back of the airplane helped to turn the airplane. The pilot moved his hips to control the wing wires and rudder.

4 The **propellers** made the airplane go forward.

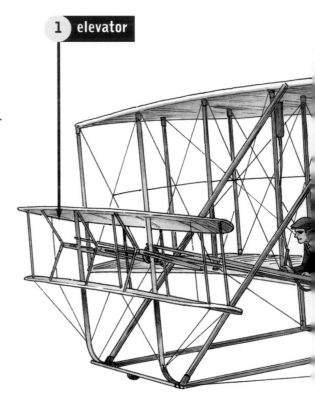

1 elevator

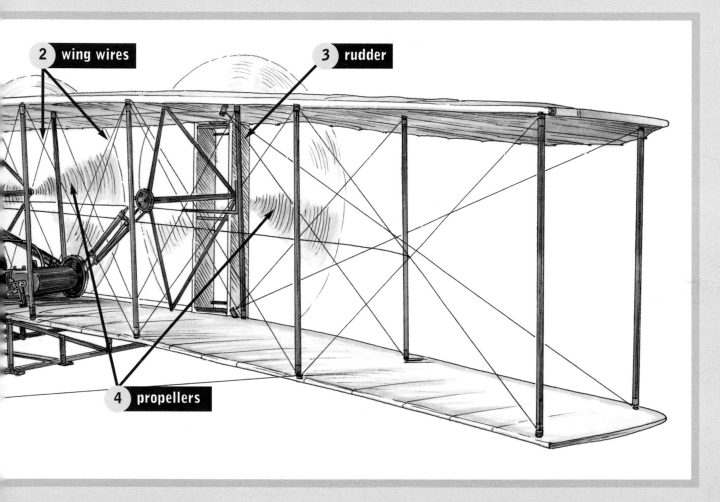

Epilogue

After their historic flights, the Wright brothers went home to Dayton. Wilbur said, "The age of flight has come at last." Wilbur and Orville continued to design and test airplanes for many years. In 1909, they built the first airplane for the United States Army.

In 1912, Wilbur died from a fever. He was only 45 years old. Orville continued their work until his death in 1948.

In 1909, the Wright brothers built an airplane for the army.

Glossary

biplane   any flying machine that has two wings

glider   an airplane without an engine; the wind helps it to fly

lever   a control stick or bar that is used to move or raise something

power   to supply with energy

propellers   strong fan-like machines that spin and make an airplane go forward

rudder   a part of an airplane that helps the pilot turn the airplane

Index